## About the Author

A creative mind should be treasured and turned into something beautiful. Cheryl has gathered up thoughts, memories and dreams and proudly turned them into heart-warming words, with the added beauty of her love for fine poetry.

# Touching Poetry

# Cheryl Anne Harris

# Touching Poetry

Olympia Publishers
*London*

**www.olympiapublishers.com**
OLYMPIA PAPERBACK EDITION

**Copyright © Cheryl Anne Harris 2023**

The right of Cheryl Anne Harris to be identified as author of
this work has been asserted in accordance with sections 77 and 78 of the
Copyright, Designs and Patents Act 1988.

A CIP catalogue record for this title is
available from the British Library.

ISBN: 978-1-80439-345-1

This is a work of fiction.
Names, characters, places and incidents originate from the writer's
imagination. Any resemblance to actual persons, living or dead, is purely
coincidental.

First Published in 2023

Olympia Publishers
Tallis House
2 Tallis Street
London
EC4Y 0AB

Printed in Great Britain

# Dedications

I wish to dedicate this book to my amazing fiancé, Paul, and my beautiful mother, for believing in me and helping me to fulfil my long-term dream.

# Acknowledgements

Thank you for believing in me.

# POEM 1: I MISS MY LIFE

I miss my home, I miss my garden, I miss my life before my independence, my freedom, and my own set of keys that once opened my very own front door.

The baking, the cooking, and the frequent neighbourly visits, they always baked a cake before they came.
The paintings I drew, the crochet I made. Yet, my hands are now crippled with pain.

I loved the birds, butterflies and bees and the occasional wasp, I didn't mind.
It's surprising what you take for granted when you're younger, as now I'm particularly blind.

I could walk for hours, come rain or shine, name that place, I would gladly walk there.
Yet now, walking three steps is completely difficult as I know life requires this wheelchair.

The treasures I had collected throughout my life surrounded me within my very own place.
Now unaware of what contents remain, as all I have left is this leather suitcase.

Some folk used to call me the rich lady that was a tale quite frequently told.
The reason behind it was not wealth at all, it was because I had a passion for all things gold.

I wore several items of jewellery and kept them in my own little secret safe place.
I never left the house without a neatly ironed blouse and not forgetting the rouge on my face.

My skin was as soft as velvet, and most gentlemen referred to me as cute.
Yet, when I look at my reflection in the mirror now, I remarkably resemble a dying fruit.

I could remember numbers off the top of my head and never once forgot my family member's birthday.
Now remembering my own birthday is harder these days as my memory is fading away.

My old friends visit me from time to time. Yet still, I feel sad and alone.
The visits are becoming less often these days as this place is so far from home.

# POEM 2: INVISIBLE WAR

This unfortunate virus that surrounds us all seems to get
stronger day by day...
So, we need to join together without touch and keep this
invisible killer at bay...

We can and will win this battle; we have proved and done it
before...
Not with this virus that is taking sad lives, but we got there and
defeated tough wars...

If we hold our heads high and help others around us and keep
on our faces that smile...
Sticking to rules and using common sense will help us reach
that extra mile...

God bless to all kind-hearted folk who are taking time out to do
extra chores.
By helping the needy, the elderly and the sick and proving their
kindness and much more.

Stop panicking, they say, yet, it's harder said than done.
But unfortunately, there is greed and folk who think for
themselves.

But trust me when I say there really are enough supplies for everyone.
Even if it's not always what you normally buy on those shelves...

When we panic, we don't think too well about the consequences and actions despaired.
You might not be aware of what actions you're taking, but we are truly making the elderly scared...

Spend a moment, morning, evening or night and think how you can maybe help another...
And hopefully, taking that little extra step in life, we will beat this invisible war together.

# POEM 3: THE 90s

You cannot say the 90s were dull, it was filled to the brim with pleasure.
An era full of excitement and smiles, a decade I will truly remember and treasure.

Jungle, trance, dance and rave boomed the nation into hardcore glistening.
The birth of hip hop, reggae and indie arrived for that more satisfaction and easy listening.

Abandoned warehouses occupied with fuelled-up folk dancing till the wake of the morning sun.
Pubs and clubs filled to the max, slowly letting them in one by one.

The Prodigy, Chemical Brothers and Fatboy Slim brought in a craze that pleased the nation.
East 17, Take That, and the Spice Girls trigged fans with eagerness and dedication.

Groups like Blur, Oasis and Suede created the indie wave
that swept through our ears.
Supergrass, Garbage, The Verve and No Doubt brought us happiness throughout these class years.

Your gorgeous Mambo No. 5 and You Get What You Give were just a few of our one-hit wonders.
Newcomers Natalie Imbruglia, Crowed House and Savage Garden hit our charts from our fellow friends down under.

Now let's talk about the drinks that surrounded us then and what we were consuming down our necks.
Kronenbourg 1664, Stella and Grolsch, not forgetting Newcastle Brown and Beck's.

Bacardi Breezers, Woodies and Hooch, VK and Smirnoff Ice. TNT Cider, 20 20 and Thunderbirds were guaranteed for fun-filled nights.

Text messages arrived with the Nokia we know well, DVD and the World Wide Web.
The Gameboy was launched, and the PlayStation was born, and that stupid Tamagotchi that messed with our heads.

Microsoft, Windows, Netflix and Amazon opened another door to our future ahead.
Mp3 Players and Satellite tv had taken over the boring books we all read.

Justin Bieber, Miley Cyrus and Ed Sheeran were born all to become famous singers one day.
Legends like Samuel J Junior, Roald Dahl and Jim Henderson sadly, unfortunately, passed away.

John Major and Tony Blair were in charge of our country; Lady Diana had a tragedy death.
We lost Michael Hutchinson, a true music legend, due to an overdose of chemicals and meth.

Frosties, Poppets, Skittles and Nerds Push Pops and toxic waste. Were sold in each of our local shops, changing a new era of confectionery taste.

Payless, Dixon's, Index and Woolworths were the best shops of the decade by far.
C&A, Select, and Topshop all favoured the revolution of the 90s wonder bra.

# POEM 4: A MOTHERS LOVE

A mother is a precious jewel, one that can't be sold.
So precious and scarce and truly treasured and is worth more
than diamonds and gold.

A mother is that guardian angel but without those flying wings.
Who sacrifices life itself to give their children those little things.

A mother's love is priceless a mother goes that much further and
beyond.
A love that's unlike any other with a truly remarkable bond.

A mother is never alone in the dark as she carries an everlasting
light.
And shows her love from the moment she wakes till the moment
she kisses us goodnight.

A mother is a powerful lady who tries her hardest in life to
succeed.
Who soldiers on through tears and pain by wearing her heart on
her sleeve.

But there is only one mother who stands out from the rest
and I'm bound to say that she is mine.
Though my growing up to my present day, she has always been
there with her torch that shines.

I love you, Mum, more than the world itself; you're remarkable, loving and dear.

A mother's day shouldn't just be a day in march but for the whole 365 days of the year.

# POEM 5: ON THE VERGE

I have never, within my whole thirty-one years, ever felt this incredibly low.
I am usually a good judge of direction and wisdom, but now finding it hard which way I should go.

This truly is a certain first for me; everywhere that I turn, there's a wall.
It won't move as it's solid; I can't climb; there're no steps, and I can't see over it because I feel that small.

Indeed I am curious to see what's lurking behind, will it mend or break my heart?
Will I go further? Should I stay where I am, or will I end up right back at the start?

There is always a coin I could toss, the head side or the unpopular tails.
But what if it was double-sided from the start, and both sides were destined to fail?

I carry four items on me, two of which are my organs that feel pain.
The pounding beat of my heart when pressure creeps in and complications of my virus confused brain.

The two other items were a hammer and rope, which I threw straight over that wall.
They were tempting devices to aid self-harm, especially when feeling so low and so small.

I shall sit here peaceful and quiet and lean against that dead end till my body and soul are at rest.
Maybe the wall is only in my virus-controlled brain, but I will follow my heart she knows best.

# POEM 6: IN MY DREAMS

It sounds like footsteps across my pillow, but I know it's the sound of my beating heart.
Where my soul and body stand back for a while, awaiting my brain to sneakily depart.

My breathing slows down, I fidget and twitch; I'm heading off into that familiar stage.
Where my brain chooses its story, its heading, its chapter, its paragraph, its words, and its page.

Unaware and unpredicted, I stumble across faces, some of which are from present to past.
I can climb trees like a gibbon and jump high like a frog and enjoy flying though so short it may last.

My stored memories and images are randomly picked from those folders that go on for miles.
Each cabinet is opened, and a tale is unfolded as she puts together pieces from my personal files.

I have no say; I'm unaware and asleep; I can't assist, contribute or look.
Whilst my body lies resting, my mind plays mischief whilst she writes another short story for her book.

One minute I'm smiling, and all is a haze and all that surrounds me is happiness and cheer.
But within a split second, I can be at the top of a cliff then my whole body is frozen with fear.

People and pets, I sadly lost over the years often return whilst I'm away in my dream.
But the sadness and heartache of waking up with them gone seems so unfair and rather extreme.

Why punish me when I'm helpless and not in control? It's not a thought; in reality, I would request.
Maybe my mind is actually making me stronger as she throws in these painful and heart-breaking tests.

Frequently I remember certain parts of my dreams but never the full story I knew that she had written.
Maybe it's a look into my future ahead, and to let on to me would be unwise and forbidden.

Maybe some memories and faces I see which are unfamiliar in a wake or a dream.
Are they passed down generations through hereditary blood, or were they born with me inside my own genes?

I generally can say that I enjoy my dreams whether they're dangerous, joyful or short.
After all, if I were always in control of my mind, they would be no dream, just another everyday thought.

# POEM 7: HIGHS AND LOWS

I love the smell of fresh bread cooking and the smell of the salty sea breeze.
I love the smell of flowers and meadows, but the pollen just makes me sneeze.

I love all insects, big and small, but then again, there is one small thing.
They either bite to steal my precious blood or impale my flesh with a sting.

I love to hang my linen to dry and to smell the fresh laundry too.
But my lovely whites all turn out shite when a pigeon releases its poo.

I wash and polish my beautiful car like it was brought right from the start.
But lazy workmen insist we finish their jobs with loose gravel; it breaks my heart.

I love the birds and the sweet tunes they sing, their tweeting from the moment it's light.
Yet, not good for my brain and my tired eyes as I'm constantly working nights.

I love all the nice fresh and spicy food, especially chicken madras.
But the morning after, oh, how I suffer when the heat comes out of my ass.

I love a pint and a shot or two to make me smile and be happy.
But I have to put up with the consequences the next day when I'm feeling awful and crappy.

I love to sit on fresh-cut grass and bask in the beautiful sun.
But tend to always sit on meadow ant hills, and in return, they bite my bum.

I love the heat from our wonderful sun, and Vitamin B has been proven to heal.
But if I relax for more than an hour out there, my skin burns and itches and peels.

I enjoy to read a book now and then but end up putting it down with frustration and bore.
As my mind is always wandering off, and I can't remember what I read on the page before.

Maybe, I over complicate little things and should banish negative thoughts that travel my head.
Or better still, just stay in my bubble and forget about leaving my bed.

# POEM 8: ONE DAY

I always said I'd never be old and never repeat what the old folks would say.
But as I slowly creep up that ladder of age, I'm using those saying more frequently today.

Back in my day, the music I treasured had melody throughout my youth years.
Now when I turn on the radio and listen to it now, it, unfortunately, tortures my ears.

Please and thank you were well know sayings everyone had good manners of some kind.
We opened doors for the old and needy and showed respect for the disabled and blind.

All roads were classed as dangerous places; we were all taught the green cross code.
We looked left; we looked right; we were cautious of cars even whilst walking those flashing cross roads.

Charity boxes outside our shops shaped like dogs with a coin slot on top.
The sound of those bottles clinking together as a van delivers us our once favourite pop.

Hello and good morning, says a familiar voice, that friendly man who opened your garden gate.
Our local dustbin man happily takes your trash even though it's most probably a job he hates.

Throughout the night, orange lights lit up pathways though not bright enough to wake tired eyes.
Now pitch black in a burglar's paradise, as the nights full of prying eyes.

Family sat together for their evening meals and spoke about what they did on that day.
Now there's no communication, and nothing is important as they just separate and go their own way.

Technology is amazing, don't get me wrong about mobile phones and face time connection.
But nobody speaks to each other about day-to-day things, which contributes to anxiety and frustration.

Kids played together in parks and streets, and we were taught never to talk to a stranger.
Now nowhere is safe from the unwanted eyes of those sickened people who thrive in danger.

I know that smoking is a danger to health, but pubs bring happiness and relaxation for sure.
It's sad when the old have to sit in the cold when once that cigarette may have helped them through the war.

It's hard to accept that I'm aging each day and that my childhood memories will soon be a thing of the past.

I can't change my future and I can't rewind time, but I shall keep my happy thoughts for as long as I last.

# POEM 9: AN UNWANTED SEED

A sharp pain hits hard right through my heart when I think how you must feel at present.
So many questions, no answers, a mind that's distorted, unaware, alone and unpleasant.

You were forced with a challenge one you could have never predicted, a serious subject that could make you hit rock bottom.
One that won't leave your thoughts from dusk till dawn, one that will make your insides feel rotten.

Why is the question, What on earth have I done? Why did I get given this awful seed?
For my life has not been an easy ride, so as for this chapter in life, I just don't need.

You wear that smile for those that surround you daily, but I know beneath there is a frightened lady.
Who pretends that the sky is a beautiful blue, but in reality, it's all grey and shady.

That giant obstacle that blocked your own life's path seemed impossible to concur and beat.
Yet, you've proved to yourself and others around you that you were the one in the driving seat.

You had that seed painfully taken away that left you weak and sore.
The life you once lived changed before your eyes with yet another set of unopened doors.

Your strength and your patience had finally shone through, and your star sign with that hard solid shell.
Coped with hours of slow treatment but conquered and defeated, as you proudly grabbed hold of that bell.

Ahead is another strange chapter, one that seems hard for me to read as I can't simply just step into your shoes.
Only you know what's right, you're a strong admiration lady, and only you can select which option to choose.

You've proved to others that once shared that boat that through that dark tunnel, it does bear the light.
It will be far from easy, and you may feel weak, but you gain nothing without jousting a fight.

Let's say fair well to this unwanted matter, for it has clung on to you long enough.
I wish to banish the days when I have looked in your eyes, knowing dam well your poorly and rough.

If I could award you a medal, it would be the most priceless one that was ever made.
It would glisten and sparkle, and shine on forever, and never Dullen, tarnish or fade.

# POEM 10: MAKE CHANGES

I wish that when I looked at people, I would smile as I would at an animal.
Devilish greedy human beings that are toxic and dangerous, and flammable.

Most often, we forget from time to time that we do share this precious earth with others.
And it slips our minds that there are other species that also have fathers and mothers.

Indeed you can call me a Hippocratic as I eat meat that once grazed the fresh fields.
I admit I add to the admissions that arise whilst being a passenger in most automobiles.

My home is cluttered with plastic, from milk to bottles of shampoo.
Even the smallest nozzles all contain that plastic, but in all fairness, there is not much I can do.

Why can't milk be produced in the glass again? Do we really nearly need all that writing in bold?
Milk is milk, and it comes from a cow and is much preferred in a glass, nice and cold.

Those plastic bags are charged for these days but often anger the stubborn tight-fisted to tears.
Are we really that slow when it comes to common sense?
Americans have used brown paper bags for years.

Why don't we have public bins any more, they were on lampposts and all round our streets.
With today's technology with those watchful eyes, surely we can stop vandalism with those simple techniques.

Build more houses, the council insists bulldoze the hillsides and trees.
Take away our wildlife's precious built homes, so they are left to starve and freeze.

Pledge two pounds a month for a poverty country is constantly aired on all of our channels.
Yet we can't donate one simple pound to vaccinate badgers, our own beautiful UK mammals.

Imagine if animals could swap places with us. Would they proudly put our heads on their trophy walls?
Would they close the doors or watch us suffer, and would they turn a deaf ear to our calls?

No one is perfect; we all have our faults, but no animal is entitled a say.
We are the weak species, we are what we are, but indeed there's always the wrong and the right way.

Leave the fish in our oceans to breed once again; take time out and try something new.
Leave the car at home and go out for a walk; you'll be surprised what that fresh air can do.

Eat what you buy, don't purchase with greed, even if you do have an experience taste.
Don't purchase to show an example of wealth when it's just sitting there going to waste.

I know times are hard and difficult these days as you don't get much for your money.
So why not create your own dish, be elaborate in the kitchen; you may find your creation quite scrummy.

We only have one chance in life and one planet, our beautiful earth.
Let's all make some small yet rewarding changes and enjoy our time for what it's worth.

# POEM 11: WHY

I don't know about you, as I haven't a clue to why silly things make me smile and giggle.
Like where does the centre of a polo mint go when the machine pops its hole in the middle?

When I've washed up, and the bowl is still full, I'm quite positive there's just water in that sink.
But as I pull that plug and it drains away, there's always a teaspoon that gives me a cheeky wink.

Ask a lady her age when she is young; it's disgraceful and as rude as can be.
Yet when there crinkled, they couldn't wait to inform you, "Did you know that I'm eighty three."

Why put sell-by dates on shampoo? You're never gonna pour the stuff down your throat.
And why, when the adverts are deafening loud, it plays hide and seek that remote.

When you're running late or in a rush, the clock always ends up acting like a jerk.
Yet, it's ten parts the hour for at least three days when you're bored and imprisoned at work.

When your head is on fire, and you reach for that box
and you need pain relief instantly bad.
Doesn't matter which side you open up first; it's always the
leaflet that comes first that you grab.

# POEM 12: WHERE HAVE YOU GONE

I always laid beside you and was always your passenger whilst in your car.
I woke every morning with that smile on my face; you were the nicest person I knew by far.

I never ever judged you on anything, you were my soul mate, my companion, my friend.
I wish to this day you could please explain why our togetherness came to this sad end.

Where have you gone? I miss you so much I can't sleep. I'm afraid and alone.
Where are my toys, my lead and bed? I'm most certainly not in my home.

I feel lost and so empty and unsure of my surroundings
all I ever see is a light and a gate.
I'm not alone in this nightmare; there are many others around me, yet they stare at me with fear and hate.

When the moon lights up the dark sky at night, that gate closes for what seems a lifetime.
And throughout the night, I lie in the dark, repeatedly hearing the howls and the wines.

I try to sleep and ignore the cries, but it's so cold I can't help it; I shake.
I pray, and I hope every night that goes by you will be there with me when I eventually wake.

I'm unsure who to blame, as I'm dazed and confused, no one to cuddle or confined or reach.
Why did you leave with my lead tied up tight to that lamppost that day on the beach?

I sat waiting for you, but you never returned, I was alone for two days and two nights.
When a stranger approached in a bright coloured van, holding a stick with a hook and a light.

He put me inside a damp cold cage with a blanket and a bowl of dried meat.
And placed me here in a much larger cage with that same blanket I still have under my feet.

When the lights switch on, and that steel gate gets unlocked there are many people that often walk by.
But no one stays long, after all, who wants a dog who just lies there and constantly cries?

Empty-handed when they walk through those gates most days but then again, that most often changes in the end.
Most days, they leave with a book and a smile with a new companion, new member, new friend.

I wanted my life to be over, I really couldn't cope with being alone.
And knowing my life would never be the same again because this old cage is now classed as my home.

Undernourished and unwell, I felt a warm hand that made me open my eyes bright one day.
A small hand had reached through and held my paw, and behind was a lady with hair so beautifully grey.

A young boy with a smile from ear to ear whispered softly to the grey-haired lady.
She did not speak nor move her hands but gave the young boy some paper all bobbly and braidly.

They turned around and walked away, but I had excitement for the first time in years.
My tail was wagging, my heart was racing and had happiness inside, not those tears.

Yet, I've been here before, and that broke my heart when I waited that day by the sea.
But suddenly, I heard laughter and then a soft giggle as a small shadow came closer to me.

A familiar face came walking through that gate, it was the man with the stick and the hook.
Yet this time was different as he whistled away carrying some candies and what seemed like a book.

He reached into his pocket and took off that old rusty lock on my cage.
The lady showed me a new collar and a shiny new lead and softly whispered, "Please don't be afraid!"

I now have the best friend ever he is so loving, so funny and kind.
Yet he can't hear my sounds or look into my eyes as he was unfortunately born deaf and blind.

I now look forward to my new life ahead and will be happy now for as long as I live.
And maybe, one day, I will see you again, but that's the life you can forget and forgive.

# POEM 13: EMOTIONS

Sometimes your body feels secure other times, you're feeling down.
It's strange how your emotions feel and confusing the way it sounds.

But even though when you're unhappy and when you're low or sad.
You will look back at all the happy times, and it doesn't seem half that bad.

There is always is a path to choose from and trying to choose which way to go.
But they all seemed rather complicated, so in which case, I shall never know.

At the moment, I am completely happy with life, love and joy.
It's like playing the game of life, winning or losing the toy.

I come that far between them, but then it all comes to an end.
I always try to amuse myself, but then again, it's just pretend.

# POEM 14: CANVAS NOT A PRINT

This wise and truthful poem is for all eyes to read and see
to understand no matter what shape or size we are, we should all
be happy with what we may be.

Mirrors themselves are variable and, believe it or not, often lie
as it's not our appearance others appreciate most, it's the inner
person that lies deep inside.

No honest person can truly say that a glance in the mirror makes
them smile.
As with all imperfections and minor alterations, they will only
keep spirits up high for a while.

A crinkle, a wrinkle, a crook in the nose, there never is hundred
per cent perfection.
So my advice to us all is to forget the outer and give the inner
self some affection.

It is individuality that indeed separates us all; not even identical
twins are the same.
Our hearts are all sizes, skeletons may vary, and only we control
those thoughts in our brains.

I say it quite often be a canvas, not a print, as there are so many fakes all around.

A print is mislaid and not often replaced, yet an oil painting will always be treasured and found.

Stand proud of what you are in life, as not one of us from birth has had an easy ride.

From puberty to losing that loved one to every droplet of tears our eyes cried.

Not everyone will appreciate the true inner of you as jealousy and hate lie within others.

But it's those folks that judge and put us down are often the shallow ones that hide under covers.

Be grateful for life every day; your eyes open through happiness and even times when you hit rock bottom.

As one day, you will be that empty shell, but your canvas remains unforgotten.

# POEM 15: CHRISTMAS

It was the night of Christmas eve, and happiness filled the air.
Where family and those loved ones showed how much they really cared.

The smiles and laughter were exciting, as there was always lots of fun.
Watching our families sipping their brandy and getting drunk one by one.

The look of the glittery paper and the fruits and nuts under the tree.
The smell of the open fire and the decorations that you would see.

As always, it was time for bed, as Santa would be arriving soon.
So off upstairs, we went into our warm and cosy room.

But of course, we didn't want to sleep, and so we gazed through our room window.
And outside was a cold and blistery night with the ground a blanket of snow.

The Lights of the streets were shining, and the houses were full of gleam.
A tiny sheet of ice had appeared upon the small and flowing stream.

Slowly our tired eyes would gently start to sleep.
And by ten or fifteen minutes, we were far away asleep.

The day we had been waiting for had finally come round.
And still, outside, there was a frost and snow laid up on the ground.

There was always a sack full of goodies on the corner of our beds.
And smiles of happiness and excitement Eagerly Whizzed around our heads.

And of downstairs, we went to see if the man himself had been.
The sherry had all been drunk and the mince pie plate was clean.

The fairy lights were twinkling, and upstairs we heard a noise.
So we waited patiently for the family to arrive to see if Santa had brought us some toys.

# POEM 16: ABOUT TIME

Spring has finally arrived again, as you can smell it within the air.
That bitter temperature is slowly heating but still chilly to the skin when bare.

Slowly the smiles upon people's faces could be seen from all around.
The tiny buds on all the shrubs and the bulbs popping their heads from the ground.

The leaves are producing rapidly upon those once naked flowing trees.
The fragrant smell of fresh linen floating around whilst washing blows in the breeze.

Holidays are being booked up and plans are going ahead.
Detoxing from that Christmas feast and hoping a few pounds are shed.

Curtains and nets always remind me of spring as it's time to wash and hang them out to air.
Then it's time to wash those windows at last to see the back of that wintery glare.

Folks churning their soil up, ready for seeds and brushing up that loose gravelled tar.
As bedding plants are settling in whilst others wash and wax their cars.

# POEM 17: THE VILLAGE

As a girl, I grew up in a small village, a quiet place by the coast
of the sea.
A friendly yet eerie part of that village to this day left a scar on
me.

It goes back to my school days when I learned a good lesson
but it wasn't by sitting in class.
It was at home in my bedroom, looking through that round
window with my eyes peering through that thin glass.

An odd little cottage that stood out from the rest, it was old and
most probably pre-war.
A strange face most day and night was always the reflection I
saw.

It's not that I was afraid of this lady it was curiosity as I knew
she lived alone.
There were never any visitors that I can remember that entered
or left that in home.

Often I would pass her in the street, but never once did she
glance up to me.
She would nip in the shop with her straw made basket and pick
up something small for her tea.

I remember one Christmas night; I bravely decided to go carol signing in the rain.
I gently tapped on her door, and to this day, remember her face pressed against that glass pane.

She was so frail and small, her face was crinkled and never once did I see her hair.
She wore an old handkerchief knotted around her neck that was floral and tattered and teared.

To this day, I can still smell her presence it was old age with a slight hint of musk.
A peculiar noticeable aroma of stale flowers with that smell of gathered dust.

Age was creeping up on me through that teenager chapter of being a *rebble*.
My dear friend and myself were out and about foolishly throwing pebbles.

All children of that age go through that stage when mischief turns into a dare.
So I picked up a rock and threw it so hard without even a thought or a care.

The sound of shattered, thin, fragile glass echoed through the streets and all around.
The village was silent with curious eyes, and rapidly my heart began to pound.

And even to now, the memories of that face still hound and haunt me today.
That look of anger, hurt and sorrow with disappointment and utter dismay.

Through my years, this lady was teased and traumatized not by myself but by many others.
It wasn't till I grew up and was old enough to understand when the truth about her came from my mother.

She explained her loss and her difficult life the old lady wasn't strange nor wild.
It was because she couldn't face up to children again due to the loss of her unborn child.

# POEM 18: DARK EVENINGS

Working away all tired and cold.
Just to earn those precious coins of gold.

Dark when I leave the house in the morning, clock out, and the sun has expired.
Oh, trust me when I say these words, I wish that I could comfortably and happily retire.

I'd bake cakes for all the old folks and those close to me, kind and dear.
And send a little note of happiness with love and a smile and a cheer.

I would gladly potter around in the garden easing my mind for hours upon hours.
Watching the life grow within my beautiful pastures and the birth of my new born flowers.

I would Stay snuggly and warm and cosy all day in my bed, all peaceful and calm.
Knowing I won't get rudely and forcefully woken by the sound of that dreadful alarm.

And wake up when I'm good and ready and plan the day ahead my way.
Instead of obeying that repetitive clock, too, in which case I have no say.

But that chapter is a long way off; I suppose I'm neither old or young in my prime.
So I'll continue to soldier on and smile, plodding along and biding my time.

The weather at present is not helping at all, for I detest the wind and the rain.
So roll on the British summer time once more so we can all raise those large smiles again.

# POEM 19: DANGER MONEY

They say money buys you happiness, but in truth, it can tear us apart.
Poisoning our inner self, unnoticeably, as it slowly eats away at your heart.

Unfortunately, greed itself can take over, and you will end up trapped behind that debt gate.
A fuel-filled emotionless living corpse enriched with no regret, no love, just hate.

Forgetting the most important things in life, all the necessary things in life we need.
Achievements, goals and future plans and the overwhelming words to succeed.

Whether you live in a mansion or a caravan, a flat, or in a box on the curbs in the town.
Money does help and indeed creates happiness, but there really is more to life than that pound.

The air we breathe, the gift of life, the family and loved ones that are always there.
Through thick and thin, penniless or broke, it just shows how much they truly do care.

# POEM 20: FADING MEMORY

I really do feel for folk with memory loss and how difficult and confusing it seems.
When our vital organs get lodged and confused between the present, the past and bad dreams.

Our human brain is so intelligent, but just like a computer, it can slowly begin to clutter.
Until it, unfortunately, starts to fade even more rapidly, disintegrating like melting butter.

You know yourself how frustrating it is when you can't remember a song or someone's name.
So to cope with that frustration from morning till night, that must drive your emotions insane.

Just like most common diseases, those hard working researches to this day still have no cure.
This is why we should contribute and continue our support, so we can further that little bit more.

We all need to have patience, a good understanding for those around us; it's not their fault and certainly not wished for or planned.
So we need to be more observant and dedicated to those who are truly grateful for that open kind hand.

There is no cure, as I mentioned before but in many ways, we can help reach that extra mile.

It's not hard nor difficult to show your devotion as in reward you're always guaranteed that smile.

We can't stop nor slow this disease down but we can ease them from Embarrassment and strife.

So, by raising our smiles and offering that kind open hand, it may help maintain a more and comfortable life.

# POEM 21: RAGDOLL

I love my dolly, my ragdoll; her name is Maisey nee.
She's by my side every morning and night ever since my grandfather gave her to me.

I remember one night, eating crusts with jam, when my papa came running through our door.
He shouted collect the children; there wasn't much time, so I grabbed Maisey nee from the floor.

My father was shouting, my mother was crying and My poor brother was nine months old.
Before I knew it, I was somewhere dark; it was damp and eerie and cold.

My father whispered to the three of us you need to be silent and not make a sound.
I heard sirens and engines and an almighty bang; then, I could feel the shaking of the ground all around.

He lit a candle, then reached into his pocket and gave me a box of what looked like coloured chalk.
And gave me a roof tile that he found on this pile, asking me to draw beautiful things and not talk.

I drew mother a flower and a big fury bee as nature fills her with happiness and content.
She misses her garden because her father joined the army before we lived in a bungalow on the outskirts of Kent.

My father disappeared, but only for a short while when he returned; he said that the coast was clear.
We climbed up two steps and out through a small hatch
I could feel mother trembling with anxiety and fear.

She tucked us up into our feather down beds, followed by good night, God bless and Lord's grace.
Holding Maisey nee as tight as can be as I pulled my covers right up over my face.

The sirens, the bangs, those bright blinding lights never once stopped through that dark and awful night.
Underground in that cold, enclosed small space like second home yet with just one room and one candle alight.

Over time as odd as it sounds, we got used to this strange way of living.
We were rationed for food along other things but had neighbours that were kind-hearted and giving.

I remember one evening, I was in the bath playing with my brother and his inflatable toys.
A bang, the room shook, I was frightened and scared and held my ears with that painful and deafening noise.

I felt bruised and looked up, I could see the lights in the sky; my bath was filled with rubble and beams.
My mother's face was frozen and stiff then she let out the most deadliest scream.

My brother was killed that sad awful night; a shell had hit our home quite hard.
And wires and trees, bricks and debris were scattered all over our own backyard.

That night was the last time I ever saw my father again, he was killed in a trench on front line.
I sadly lost my mother due to complicated health and certainty learned that a broken heart needs time.

My family has passed, yet I've slowly moved on and still treasure that small part of me.
For I have the best gift that was given with love, my own rag dolly, my old Maisey nee.

# POEM 22: OLD ROAD

In the west midlands, there's Warwickshire; it's full of little towns, some of which are discreet.
But there is legendary history with a roman road, and it goes by the name Watling street.

Two hundred and seventy miles of the cobbled road began its journey in the eighteen hundreds, a long straight road.
That can tell a story vital for delivering those essential goods.

This Anglo-Saxon medieval road is also known on a map of the A5 with a haunting past that could tell many sad tales of when those bloody battles of this road came alive.

The beginning is at Marble Arch in London, which was being built in 1872.
And in wales lies Admiral Arch, which is the actual end of that long road too.

Along Watling street, itself were many taverns, inns and bars.
Railway stations and train tracks galore, it was uncommon to actual own cars.

Just a slight turning off the long pebbled road within an alehouse, a stranger was lurking.
In a local pub called the cat at sibson, a highwayman who goes by the name Dick Turpin.

If you were to dig deep down along Watling street, you might be surprised by what you may find.
As that original cobbled road lies underneath, as well as many roman artefacts of some kind.

A village just off that miles-long road in Mancetter where the hills raise higher.
Lies a dark tale of the death of the legend Boudica who was the lady of the Roman empire.

Many villages with stately built mansions and halls and farms filled with livestock and hay.
And with the views from the peak of the Merrivale Abbey Malvern hills can be seen on a crisp clear day.

# POEM 23: LIDL

Working at Lidl has opened my eyes to the folk that is ignorant
and rude.
Whether it's Monday morning or the sky is still blue, they
purchase their goods in a mood.

Children today are really bone idle as they stare at their
struggling mums.
Light-fingered kids with an attitude disorder and those fools
with insufficient funds.

How many times do we tell our customers that our baskets
shouldn't leave the store?
And our lovely bakery, being manhandled daily, use the tongs;
that's what they're God dam for.

We're going too fast, we're going too slow, for God's sake,
make up your mind.
Just smile and be happy, Lidl is not bad, and our products are
honest and kind.

If you've brought every item we have in our shop, and the belt
is full to the brim.
Let the person behind grab their items so small don't be rude
and refuse to let them in.

# NOT POETRY, BUT OTHER WORK I DO

# FAMOUS NAMES

Jack got his own knife
Talks crap and owns a hammer and a trolley
Alan owns his own set of keys
How the hell did Lorraine get her own quiche recipe
Stanley got his blades
Why has Bob got a cat
How did Dave get his own channel
Why did Henry become a hoover
How come Martin chose a house over a flat
Who gave Harry his chip shop
Why does Hillary make blinds
What made Larry so happy
What's so even about Steven
Who gave Tommy that gun
Jeys got his own clothes, not to mention his own fluid
Why has Pete stop selling his soil
Why do all the screw drivers belong to Philip
Has Jacob really has gone crackers
Is Christian truly religious
Is frank really that minted
Marigold has been keeping our hands soft for years
How does Victoria make such a light sponge
Why is Matt always at the front door
Is Simon really that simple
Why is Tim so tiny

How come Austin stopped making the Alegro
Terry's nappies were so unhygienic
Where the hell has Charlotte's web gone
What type of apple was Adam
What's so dirty about Diana
Is William really that sweet
Whys Jerry got his own can
And is Laurel a true evergreen
Does Harvey actually make beds
Does Perry always have to be sparkling
Why should I need to talk to Frank
And who gave Bill his board
Does joe always talk B*******
And has anyone got Regs number

# POEM 24: OLD GERALD

Old Gerald was a dirty old bugger; his bones were fragile and weak.
He was dying for some sexual pleasure, but he could never reach his high peak.

He tried magazines and videos, but nothing would do the trick.
He just sat around saying bleeding hell as he looked at his shrivelled up prick.

Now Gerald had a lovely lady wife who went by the name of June Jilly.
She was happy with Gerald and the way that he was and often told him to stop being rather silly.

Gerald raided his bank and his savings, and in all honesty, he had already got a fair Bob.
So he booked himself into a gentleman's clinic to finally get an enlarged and fatter knob.

Gerald woke up from his operation feeling tender, sore and confused.
With his manhood like a deformed parsnip and his balls that were the size of balloons.

Unfortunately, the operation was unsuccessful, spoke the doctor with a sad look on his face.
Gerald lifted the covers up and pointed and said well, that things are a bloody disgrace.

Poor Gerald got up from bed in a rage and said right, I'm off out for a fag.
And went waddling off through the hospital doors, and trailing behind was a full catheter bag.

Now Gerald was not a fan of mod cons and swore never to own a mobile phone.
So with a fag in one hand and a bag of piss in the other poor Gerald had no option but to walk home.

"What the bloody hell are you doing, you fool," said a sharp and familiar voice.
It was Frank, his nosey neighbour next door and his fat wife, whose name, by the way, was Joyce.

Now, this Frank was an odd clumsy character and was also well known for his rather short fuse.
And Joyce was chubby with a red veiny nose and always smelt of hairspray bleach and booze.

Blimey, he said to our Gerald, you must be mad, in pain and bloody sore.
As he helped Gerald into the back of his car, slamming his catheter bag right inside the door.